The Scholarship Club Guide II
Finding Applying and Winning Scholarships and Academic Awards
© 2015 The Scholarship Club FPC
855-469-3322   www.TheScholarshipClub.com

Table of Contents

START YOUR SCHOLARSHIP PLAN 1

FOLLOW THROUGH 2

COMMON SCHOLARSHIP MYTHS 3

COMPLETING SCHOLARSHIP APPLICATIONS 14

YOUR SCHOLARSHIP APPLICATION KIT 15

YOUR PERSONAL STATEMENT 16

YOUR ACADEMIC RESUME 22

LETTERS OF RECOMMENDATION 24

THANK YOU STATEMENTS 30

CONTINUE BUILDING YOUR SCHOLARSHIP TOOL KIT 31

    SAMPLE TRANSCRIPT 32

LOCATE SCHOLARSHIPS 41

SET SCHOLARSHIP GOALS 42

EVALUATING SCHOLARSHIP OPPORTUNITIES 44

RANKING SCHOLARSHIP OPPORTUNITIES 48

    THE SCHOLARSHIP CLUB™ 56

    CLASS LEVERAGE SHEET 56

    CLASS TOPIC: US ECONOMY 56

BUILD YOUR SCHOLARSHIP TEAM **58**

    COMMUNITY SERVICE LOG 59

        List the duties you performed and what you learned 59

THE SCHOLARSHIP CLUB **60**

    LEADERSHIP ACTIVITY LOG 60

LOCATE SCHOLARSHIPS ONLINE **61**

WORKING WITH A SCHOLARSHIP COACH **65**

CONTESTS AND COMPETITIONS **68**

    COLLEGE VISIT FORM 72

GET CAREER SMART **78**

A WORD ABOUT THE DEEP WEB **79**

OUTSTANDING SEARCHES **80**

OPENSOCIAL AND WEB 2.0 .... **81**

MORE SITES **82**

RESOURCES FOR MINORITY/DIVERSE STUDENTS **83**

RESOURCES FOR STUDENT ATHLETES AND PARENTS **85**

RESOURCES FOR STUDENTS WITH DISABILITIES **86**

ABOUT THE SCHOLARSHIP CLUB FPC **88**

Start Your Scholarship Plan

Applying for scholarships is not hard, but it takes planning. With a few hours of work, you can plan your homework assignments to coordinate with essay contests, plan your science projects to coordinate with science competitions, and plan your math assignments to coordinate with a national math essay competition.

A large part of winning scholarships involves being organized and being prepared. This tool will give you the tools and worksheets you need to track important scholarship dates, set goals for winning, and follow-up after you win. The most important part of this entire process is your ability to follow through.

Follow Through

You must be very diligent in following through with requesting information, with mailing your applications on time, and with asking questions when you are not sure what to do next. Following through is one skill you will not get from reading any book or attending a seminar – you just have to do it. The Scholarship Club helps students every year apply for dozens of scholarships. The three key things we see that separate students who win a lot of scholarships from students who win a few scholarships are:

1. The ability to plan the work
2. The ability to organize the dates
3. The ability to follow through with commitments

By learning winning scholarship application techniques and mastering the three key areas above you'll see results from your effort – scholarship winnings! Let's get started.

Common Scholarship Myths

There are a lot of myths about winning scholarships floating around. Let's take a moment to talk about them, and I'll tell you why they are not true. At the Scholarship Club we expose the top 10 myths about winning scholarships and tell you what you can do to overcome them. The most popular myths about winning scholarships are:

- You must have excellent grades
- Scholarships are only for high school seniors
- No one really wins scholarships
- You must be in a lot of clubs and organizations
- You have to be a "star" athlete to win athletic scholarships
- You must have significant financial need to win scholarships
- You should apply for every scholarship you can find
- It's hard to find scholarships
- Applying for scholarships is just like apply to college
- There's nothing you can do to improve your chances of winning

Before we go any further, let's take a moment to debunk each of these myths.

Myth 1: You Must Have Excellent Grades

Truth: You don't need a 4.8 GPA (Grade Point Average) to win scholarships. Most scholarships are awarded for things you do now, things you want to do in the future, or things you've done in the past. Students win scholarships for:

Current/Future Major: *What do you want to study? Have you chosen a major?*

Future Career: *What do you want to be when you grow up? What type of work will you do after graduation?*

Leadership: *Have you participated in organizations?*

Athletics: *Do you play sports for fun? Are you on a team? What sports have you played?*

Service/Volunteerism: *What do you like to do to help others?*

Hobbies: *Do you like to play music? Are you a chess master?*

Ethnicity: *Are you or your parents from a country other than the USA?*

Religion: *Do you have a specific faith or belief?*

Ability: *Have you overcome a difficulty during your life?*

Parent's Employers: *Ask your parents about the employee groups at work.*

Need: *Financial need is usually recognized by scholarship committees.*

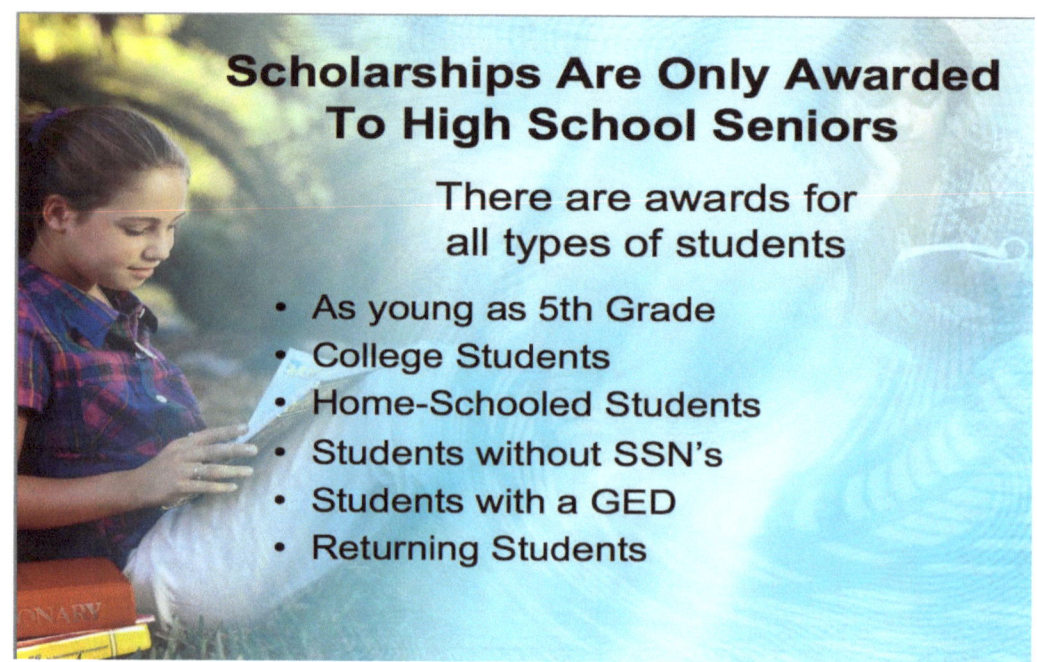

Myth 2: Scholarships Are Only for High School Seniors

Truth: Scholarships are awarded to students at all grade levels, even for kindergartners! At the Scholarships Club we work with students, starting in grade 5, to apply and win scholarships, essay contests, and academic awards. We list a whole section on scholarships for young student later in this eBook. Here are some examples of the types of scholarships students are winning as early as middle school:

•VFW Youth Essay - $10k	-7/8th Grade
•Dupont Science Challenge - $3k	-9th Grade
•Voice of Democracy Contest - $30k	-10th Grade
•Ayn Rand Essay Contest - $10k	-11th Grade
•Gates Millennium Scholarship – $FT	-12th Grade
•ASIST – $2500	-Non-Traditional Students
Jack Kent Cook - $30,000	-Transfer Students
•Tylenol Scholarship - $10k	-Undergraduate Students
•Hertz Foundation Fellowship - $33k	-Graduate Students
Netflix PhD Full Tuition and Stipend	-PhD Students

Myth 3: No One Really Wins Scholarships

Truth: Ordinary students just like you are winning scholarships every day!

The truth is: you can't win if you don't apply. Since 2008, members of the Scholarship Club won scholarships in just about every category:

- ✓ $2,500 won by a returning student
- ✓ $50,000 won by a transfer student
- ✓ $20,000 won by an undergraduate student
- ✓ $30,000 won by a graduate student

Some of the scholarships won by Scholarship Club members since 2008:

- ❒ The Gates Millennium Scholarship
- ❒ Delta Sigma Theta Scholarship
- ❒ Omega Psi Phi Scholarship
- ❒ Ronald McDonald House Scholarship
- ❒ The Claremont Links Scholarship
- ❒ The NAUW Scholarship
- ❒ National Merit Scholarship
- ❒ University Music Scholarships

Scholarship Club meetings are where you will learn to find scholarships, how to apply for scholarships, and what to do after you win them.

Myth 4: You Must Join
A Lot of Clubs and Organizations

Truth: You do not have to join every club on campus to be eligible to win scholarships! Make sure that the clubs and organizations that you belong to are meaningful to you, and be prepared to say why. Scholarship judges want to know how you served in the organizations; they look at your contribution. Make sure that you participate in clubs because you desire meaningful involvement. Show that you've invested in the organization by holding an office or leading an effort. Remember, you don't have to be president of the club to be considered a leader; heading-up a fundraising drive shows leadership too.

Discussion Questions

What clubs do you plan to join?

Why will you join those clubs?

Myth 5: You Must Be A "Star" Athlete to Win Athletic Scholarships

Truth: Athletic related scholarships go to students who are able to write about being an athlete. The truth is being good at one school doesn't mean that you can't be great at another school! Have you heard of the SAMMY Award? SAMMY stands for Scholar Athlete Milk Mustache of the Year, and this award goes to athletes who can write about how playing sports has helped them in life (and how milk has helped them too). There are very many essay contests and academic awards available to students who play sports, not just the top athletes.

Discussion Questions

What sports do you participate in?

Is there a sport you are interested in learning?

Myth 6: You Must Have Significant Financial Need to Win Scholarships

Truth: There are basically two categories of scholarships; need based and merit based.

Need Based Scholarships depend on the students financial status. If your family earns under a certain amount of money (which varies) then you can qualify for need based scholarships. Students and their families must demonstrate financial need to win these Scholarships.

Merit Based Scholarships depend on the other things we talked about in the first myth. These scholarships are based on your achievements, your skills, your interests and your talents. There are a lot more merit based scholarships and academic awards that you'd think!

Myth 7: You Should Apply For Every Scholarship You Can Find

Truth: Make sure that the scholarships you apply for are a Good Fit for you
Be selective about the scholarships you apply for. We encourage you to apply for a lot of scholarships, just make sure that those scholarships are right for you. Make sure that the organization holds the same values that you do, that the scholarship is related to something that you care about.

Prioritize the scholarships you will apply for. Look at the number of awards giving, the amount of the award, the award due dates, and your available time. Later in this eBook we'll show you the 10 steps to evaluating any scholarship opportunity. Use these steps with the worksheet to make sure that you are using your time wisely and applying for the best scholarships for you. Learn to automate your scholarship search. We will talk about this more later.

Myth 8: It Is Hard To Find Scholarships

Truth: By now you know that this myth isn't true.

Finding scholarships is easier today than it was 10 years ago. Finding scholarships is actually easy when you know where to look. With the scholarship club you will learn to look for scholarship opportunities online, in books and magazines, even at your school. Most importantly - you should not pay for Scholarship Information. We will register for free scholarship databases, discuss how to get scholarship information from the Career Center at your school, and how to find scholarships through your Chamber of Commerce. At the Scholarship Club, we believe that finding scholarships is the easy part; it's completing the application that requires the most work.

Discussion Questions

What scholarship databases will you subscribe to?

What is the name of the person who runs the Career Center at your school?

Myth 9: Applying For a Scholarship Is Similar To Applying To College

Truth: Applying for a scholarship is more work than applying to some colleges.

Applying for scholarships takes more work. You must study the scholarship grantors' organization; know their mission statement. Research past winners, even (sometimes) research who is on the scholarship committee! College applications tell you exactly what the college is expecting from you. Colleges and universities send you nice, glossy, color brochures that show you what's important to them. You'll have to go to the website to research the scholarship granting organization, they don't tell you much about the winners or the follow-up work that the winners had to do to receive the scholarship. Applying for scholarships is good preparation for applying to college or university.

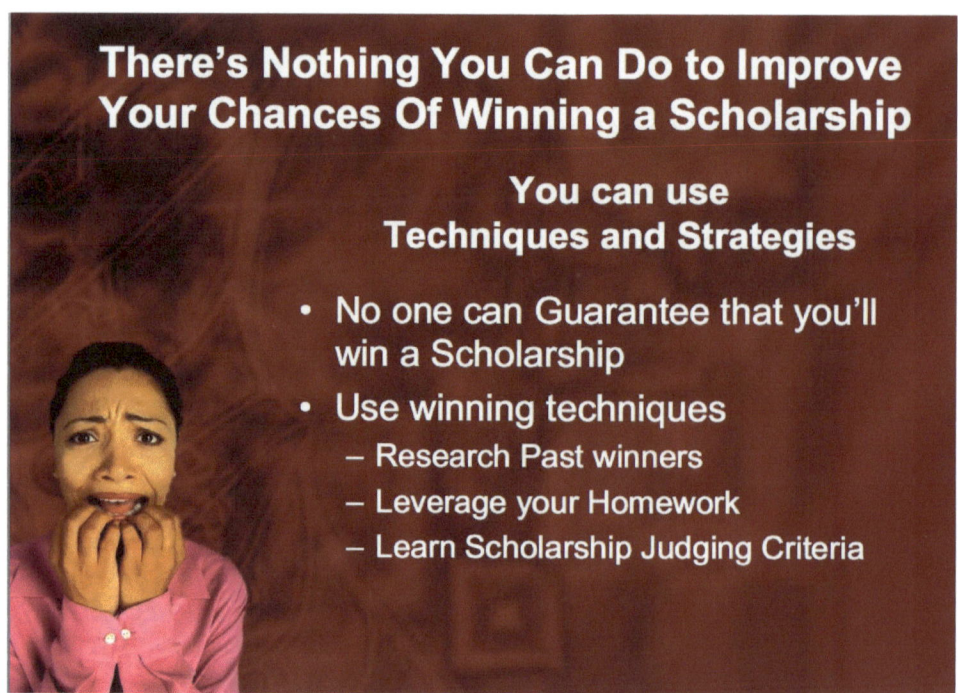

Myth 10: There Is Nothing You Can Do To Improve Your Chances Of Winning a Scholarship

Truth: You can improve your chances of winning a scholarship by using the techniques of scholarship winners. Scholarship winners know that scholarship judges are looking for. They know that scholarship judges place value on:

- ❒ Hard Work
- ❒ Teamwork
- ❒ Initiative
- ❒ Responsibility
- ❒ Purpose
- ❒ Overcoming Obstacles
- ❒ Perseverance
- ❒ Passion and Enthusiasm
- ❒ Civic Duty
- ❒ Character

Scholarship winners know how to work smarter, not just harder. They leverage their homework; use homework assignments to win scholarships. It's not as hard as you'd think. Try matching an essay contest with an essay you have to write for your English class. You will get double the payoff for doing the work one time.

Completing Scholarship Applications

Finding scholarships in the 21st century is easy; winning scholarships takes WORK. That is good news for you! If you are willing to put in the work, you can win scholarships and academic awards, if you do not put in the work you will not win. . In fact, you can win the money you need to attend college before you finish high school! All you have to do is get smart about winning and prepare to apply. Winning scholarships means understanding how to use the opportunities available to you right now, right where you are. You need to know the five "W's" and an "H":

- **Who** to ask for recommendations
- **What** scholarship judges want
- **Where** to find scholarships
- **When** to ask for help
- **Why** a Personal Statement is important
- **How** to structure your Autobiographical Essay

The best part about winning scholarships is that you can learn the techniques. Most scholarships reward students for performing community service, writing essays, talking about future goals, or describing what you think the future will bring. Imagine winning $500 just for writing about your own ideas!

At Scholarship Club meetings, you will learn ways to **leverage** completing homework with applying for academic contests. For example, suppose you have to write an essay about world peace for your history class. You can research current essay contests on that topic, write your class-assigned paper, turn it in, ask your teacher to "correct" it for you, and then submit the paper to an essay contest. You can complete your class assignment, get a good grade, and win a cash award for "doing your homework."

Your Scholarship Application Kit

Get ready to win scholarships by assembling your Scholarship Application Kit - your SAK. Your SAK contains the items you need to start applying right now. Build your Scholarship Kit on piece at a time – do not skimp on this part. The four most important pieces you need in your SAK are:

1. Your personal statement
2. Your academic resume
3. Letters of recommendation
4. Thank you statements

The next few pages will walk you through the process of assembling your SAK. Let's get started!

Your Personal Statement

Your personal statement the only part of your application over which you have full control.

- Your academic record is what it is
- Your extracurricular activities are in the past
- Your recommendation letters are from others
- Your test scores depend on your performance on that day

Scholarship committees look for specific things in a personal statement. You will want to make sure that your personal statement shows off your creativity, your curiosity, pride in your work, your enthusiasm for learning, or your capacity for teamwork. Your personal statement should be thoughtful and honest. It demonstrates that you have put thought into your future, gained a clear perspective on your experiences, and decided what you want for your future. It gives the reader a vivid and compelling picture of you--in essence, telling the reader what he or she should know about you.

Your personal statement should be about 250 to 300 words long. It should tell what is important to you and discuss your goals. Your personal statement should have a catchy introduction that will keep the reader interested. It should demonstrate your knowledge of the Scholarship/major/college. Above all, your personal statement should exude confidence. Use your personal statement to highlight your initiative and ability to overcome obstacles.

Begin writing your personal statement by brainstorming. Brainstorming is the first stage of writing, often called "prewriting." Brainstorming is the process of gathering all of your ideas and getting them on paper without editing them. The brainstorming stage does not involve editing, so do not censor your ideas. There will be enough time to edit later; right now, you want to get all of your ideas down so that you do not forget anything.

Brainstorming is NOT an outline, NOT a draft and certainly NOT an essay. The purpose of brainstorming is to write out ideas, thoughts, pieces of thoughts, without regard for their connections with each other. Structure and form are not important at this point. What is important is to get everything out of your head and onto paper. Read the statements below. Take time now to write the responses to these statements. Try to write at least three items for each statement.

What are my strengths?
What are my weaknesses?
What is special about me?
What kind of person am I?
What do I care about most?
Why is (BLANK) more important to me than (BLANK)? (Fill in the blanks.)
What is it like growing up in (BLANK)?
What is it like going to school at (BLANK)?

Next, use the information you have uncovered through brainstorming to address the following topics:

An achievement that made me feel terrific about myself is
_____

Something I have struggled to overcome or change about my life or myself is
_____
_____

An event or experience that taught me something about myself is
_____
_____

A "real drag" of an experience that I had to get past was
_____
_____

Someone's act of strength or courage that affected me was
_____

A family experience that influenced me in some powerful way
_____

A lesson, class project, activity or job that had an impact on my academic or career goals was _____

One time I blew it, failed, made bad choices was _____
_____

Some memorable event or advice involving an older person was _____
_____

An event that helps to define myself, in terms of my background is
_____

Next, choose one or two of your favorite responses from the list you created. Make sure your written description addresses the following three questions.

1. What were the key moments and details of the event?

2. What did I learn from this event?

3. What aspect of this event stays with me most?

Now, decide on a theme for your Personal Statement. Use the experience you wrote about above to answer the following questions:
What does this event reveal about me?

What makes it special or significant?

How does this event make me special or make me stand out?

What truth about me was revealed through this event?

You are probably wondering if there are more things that you should know about writing your personal statement. Yes, there are a few more things. Writing a good personal state is:

- ♦ A long process
- ♦ Can take 10 to 12 drafts
- ♦ Can take 2 months
- ♦ Uniquely "You"

Do not wait to start your personal statement, start now. Remember that your statement will change as you experience new things, so be prepared to update it every year.

Your Personal Statement DRAFT starts here

Your Academic Resume

Creating an academic resume is not hard; it is pretty much just writing about yourself, with just a few words. The top of your academic resume should display:

- Your first and last name/ address/ phone and email
- The name of the school you attend
- Your college entrance test scores (if you have them)
- Your Grade Point Average (GPA)

Next, the body of your Academic Resume should share more information about you. This part of your AR should list:

- Your activities
- Your volunteer experience
- Your work experience
- Any awards or honors you've received

Before you create your actual academic resume, take some time to write this information down on a sheet of paper. This will help you identify what information you already have, and the information you need to "research." You may have to find copies of awards you have received, look at your transcript for the courses you have taken, or even ask your parents to help you remember some volunteer experience. Your Academic Resume can display your teamwork, responsibility and civic duty.

The next page shows an example of an Academic Resume. I created this example by using a template in my word processing software. You can create your AR this way, or you can buy a resume making software package at any office supply store. Another option is to check the Internet free resume making templates; its fast and the free templates usually work well.

Sample Academic Resume

Your Address   City   State   Zip Code
Your Phone Number   Your Email Address   Your LinkedIn Address

Education

Your High School Name   City, State
Graduation: Put Date Here
G.P.A: Put It Here if it's really good
Test Scores: Here if you have them

Activities

Sports   *Pasadena HS*
Participated as a team member from 2005-2006. Played wide receiver, safety, linebacker, punt, kickoff, kickoff-return, and defensive end.

Pasadena HS
Participated as a contributing team member from 2004-2005. Competed in 110-meter low hurdles, 300-meter hurdles, 4 x 200 relay, 4 x 400 meter relay, 2-mile event.

Villa Park, Pasadena
Participated in Villa Park boxing program. Achieved endurance and strength development while learning life-enhancing skills.

Performing Arts   *Pasadena, CA*
Played drums for the Roughriders band. Performed at many venues including Martin Luther King Day parade in Pasadena.

Extra-Curricular School Activity   *Pasadena, CA*
Participated in the ROP program at Rose City High school. Learned interviewing skills and workplace etiquette.

Work Experience

Subway Sandwiches   *Pasadena, CA*
Performed various duties as required. Worked as a Cashier and performed food preparation.

Volunteer Experience

Humane Society   *Pasadena, CA*

Fed and brushed dogs and cats that were brought to the Humane Society.

Letters of Recommendation

Getting great letters of recommendation can be a project of its own. In the Scholarship Club, we recommend that our members collect 20 letters of recommendation. Most scholarships will only require one or two letters.

A great letter is so specific and detailed that it seems to have been written only for you. It will include revealing stories or anecdotes that illustrate how you have exhibited certain positive qualities. A great letter refers to specific incidents and occasions. Details make your recommendation letter appear genuine and the reader can tell that you are memorable to the person writing the letter. A great letter distinguishes itself by making bold statements that judges will know were not written for just anyone.

Start by developing a list of people who can write a good letter of recommendation for you. Record how well the person knows you and what aspects of your life this person can write about. Good candidates for writing letters of recommendation are:

- ☐ Teachers
- ☐ Professors
- ☐ School Administrators
- ☐ Counselors
- ☐ Employers
- ☐ Coaches
- ☐ Activity advisors
- ☐ Clergy
- ☐ Customers
- ☐ Family Friends

The Scholarship Club
Sample Recommendation Request Letter

Dear Mr. Jones,
Thank you for agreeing to write a letter of recommendation for me.

As we discussed, your recommendation letter is part of a scholarship application I am submitting for _____, a scholarship program that seems designed to recognize someone like me. The program seeks to award scholarships of varying amounts to students who exhibit excellence in _____. (Extracurricular activities)

One of the important areas I am highlighting on my application is the _____ abilities/responsibilities and skills and how such duties/abilities have had a positive impact on my school and community. As _____ (my counselor), I thought you would be an excellent person to comment on these aspects of my extracurricular involvement. Of special interest to the _____ Scholarship committee are activities and projects such as:

- The community food and clothing drive I helped organize for the past three years
- The student government fundraising program I recently initiated which has already raised more than $9,000 for school-sponsored clubs
- My representation of your school on the city youth violence task force

The application materials also request that you comment on the personal qualities I have exhibited through these projects. As additional background information, I have attached a list of my extracurricular projects, with the ones directly related to _____ in bold. Since the deadline for postmarking materials is _____, it would be great if I could pick up your recommendation letter (for inclusion with the rest of my application) two weeks from this Wednesday. Your letter can be addressed to the "_____Scholarship Awards Judging Committee."

Again, thank you so much for all your time and energy spent in writing this recommendation for me. I really appreciate your efforts to help in my quest to secure much-needed scholarship funds, and I am especially grateful for all the help and guidance you have shown me during the year. If you have any questions, feel free to contact me at _____ (phone number).

Sincerely,

Ernest Student

Start the recommendation process by identifying all of the people you will consider asking for a letter. Be sure to include teachers, counselors, youth leaders, and those with whom you volunteer. You do not want to get a letter of recommendation from a close relative (like your mother) because that person can seem biased.

Recommender Name

Next, write down how long you have known the recommender. List exactly how you know them; is this person your scout leader for the past 3 years? After you identify who they are and how you know them, write down what type of letter they can write based on knowing you. Is this person your math teacher who can write about you academic ability? Is this person a youth leader who can write about your community service? Is this person a peer who can write about your leadership ability?

Known how long?

How do I know this person?

Review the themes from your personal statement or autobiographical essay. What aspect of your personality can this person write about? If you completed it, review the examples you listed in the Themes section of your autobiographical essay tool. Is this person in any of your examples? Perhaps this person can write about your character or trustworthiness. Write down the topic you believe this person can write about.

What aspect/theme can this person write about me?

Keep careful track of this information. You may want to write this information in a diary or journal. You can use a sheet or two of paper to keep up with this information. On the next page you will find a sample recommender template that you can copy and use to keep track of your recommendation letter writers.

Recommender Name	Known how long?	How do I know this person?	What aspect/theme can this person write about me?

It is very important that you communicate effectively with those who are writing letters of recommendation for you. Make sure that you give them all of the materials that they will need to write a great letter for you. Always ask for a letter of recommendation formally; enclose a written request for the letter. Be sure to include your academic resume and your personal statement when you request a letter of recommendation.

You will want to give your recommender plenty of time to write the letter. It is best to ask for a recommendation several weeks before you need it. At the Scholarship Club, we recommend that you ask for both a hard copy and a soft copy of any letters you need. Having the letter in different formats will make it easy to return to your letter writer when you need an updated letter later.

It is ok to give your letter writer "Talking Points." In your request to them, only include topics about the scholarships that you want them to address. If the letter writer is a teacher, ask them to talk about your achievement as a student. If the letter writer is a community leader that you know well, ask them to write about your responsibility and civic duty. Communicate with your letter writer by giving them a roadmap. Think of your request for a letter of recommendation like driving directions - it gives the recommender a roadmap of where you need them to go, but they choose how fast to go, where to take rest stops, and what radio station to listen to. Be tactful as you give them "talking points." You do not want to seem as if you are telling them what to write.

Discussion Question:
Why should you give a roadmap to your recommendation letter writer?

Thank You Statements

Whenever you receive a letter of recommendation, you should always say "Thank You." There are many ways to say "Thanks for helping me out", but the most important thing is that you say it. I recommend sending a Thank You card, but you may find it more convenient to send a Thank You email. If this person really went beyond in giving you great recommendations, or if you will have to ask them for several letters, I suggest you include a small gift along with the card or email. Here is an example of a Thank You response that you can use as a guide:

Dear _____
Thank you for taking time to write on my behalf. I appreciate your effort and support throughout my application process. I will keep you updated on my progress and let you know the final result. Again, thank you so much for believing in me.

Sincerely,
Earnest Student

Continue Building Your Scholarship Tool Kit

Your Scholarship Tool Kit is unique to you and you alone; think of it as a custom view of YOU. You Scholarship Tool Kit should contain:

A copy of your Transcript
An Autobiographical Essay
Log of leadership activities
A Log of Community Service Activities
Monthly Goal Sheets
A Personal Statement
Your Scholarship Tracking Tool

Preparing means assembling these documents **BEFORE** you begin applying for scholarships. Let's start by getting a copy of your transcript.

Your Transcript

You can get an unofficial copy of your transcript from your school principal or counselor by asking for it. The best way to approach this is to make an appointment with your counselor. During your appointment, tell your counselor that you are preparing to apply for scholarships and you need a copy of your transcript. You do not really need to tell your counselor that you are applying for scholarships to get your transcript, but it is a good idea. Your counselor is probably someone you will ask for a letter of recommendation. By making an appointment and talking about scholarship applications, you are sort of giving the counselor a "heads-up." You can even let your counselor know that you will be asking for a recommendation soon.

A Sample Transcript

Your Autobiographical Essay

Creating your autobiographical essay takes some work, but it is worth it. I recommend working on this type of essay as an assignment for your English class, or taking a workshop to help write it. With that said, I will tell you how we recommend starting your autobiographical essay.

First, you should understand what scholarship judges look for in applicants. You have reviewed the Scholarship Judging Criteria, by now you should be able to identify a few themes that describe the type of person you are, or your accomplishments. Use 2 – 3 themes that feel comfortable. Here is a list of the most commonly used themes when writing an autobiographical essay.

A good person doing good things
A creative and talented person
A survivor of a difficult situation
A really smart person
A political activist
An athlete
A scientist
An entrepreneur
A good leader

As you select the themes you want to use in your autobiographical essay, think of a story or example from your life that demonstrates the theme. Perhaps you designed your own pattern for a handbag (creative), or maybe you are the person everyone comes to for advice (leader). Make sure that you write about a specific example when you discuss the theme in your essay. Your autobiographical essay can highlight your passion and enthusiasm, as well as your sense of purpose. Next, follow the steps in the Personal Statement section.

Crafting Your Autobiographical Essay
Theme Sheet 1

Theme: Good person doing good things

Your example(s)

Theme: Creative and Talented

Your example(s)

Theme: The Survivor

Your example(s)

Theme: The "Brain"

Your example(s)

Theme: The Activist

Your example(s)

Crafting Your Autobiographical Essay
Theme Sheet 2

Theme: The Entrepreneur
Your example(s)

Theme: The Leader
Your example(s)

Theme: The Scientist
Your example(s)

Theme: The Athlete
Your example(s)

Theme:
Your example(s)

After you have taken time to answer these questions, you are ready to start writing your essay. The structure of your autobiographical essay should follow the basic structure of any good essay.

- An introductory paragraph with a theme
- 2-4 body paragraphs that develop your theme
- The final paragraph will contain your most poignant information
- A conclusion that widens the lens and wraps up your autobiographical essay

An introductory paragraph should provide your essay's main theme. Your introduction is where you establish the tone of your autobiographical essay. This is where you set the scene, define its theme, and generally hook your reader by sparking interest with details and quotes. It is important that you get right to the point. Be sure, too, that your language is clear and specific – do not use filler words or clichés. Most importantly, be sure that the introductory paragraph captures the main idea of your essay.

Sometimes the introduction is the last part of the personal statement to be completed, and that is okay. The introduction should provide a snapshot of what the rest of the essay will develop and expand upon, so if you do not know where the rest of the essay is headed, the introduction is impossible to write. Therefore, it is important to outline your essay so that you know how each of your examples will build upon one another. Use between two and four body paragraphs to develop your theme by using examples and detailed experiences that build upon each other. The final body paragraph should contain your most important information. Body paragraphs are the meat of your essay, which makes them the most important part of your essay. In the body, paragraphs expand on and provide support for the theme you introduced in the first paragraph and will provide the details that move that theme forward. A two-page essay will typically contain 2-4 body paragraphs. Each paragraph should have:

- A topic sentence that expands your theme and makes a transition from the paragraph before
- Developed ideas that support your essay's theme
- An ending sentence that wraps-up the paragraph and helps to transition into the next paragraph

The first paragraph is where you start building a support for your theme. This is where you begin with the smallest components of your theme and, in following paragraphs, work toward the most significant paragraphs. Another option is to organize your events chronologically, in the order that they happened. Try both methods and see which one is most persuasive for your theme.

Your conclusion should widen the lens and wrap up your essay without summarizing or repeating what you already wrote. Your conclusion is your chance to extend you main points. Use the conclusion to demonstrate how significant your experience is, in a larger context. Remember, <u>your conclusion is not a repeat</u> or summary of ideas presented earlier in the essay or application. Instead, your conclusion should re-affirm your essay's theme. This means that your conclusion should "widen the lens" rather than "narrow the focus."

Sometimes students just repeat in the essay the same information that is in the scholarship application. **Do not do this!** Remember, your reader already knows from reading your application, for example, that you are in the California Scholarship Federation and a member of the Ethnic Studies Club. What the reader does not know is why you chose to participate in these activities and how your involvement in these activities shows your particular interests and talents-- your essay's theme. If one of these experiences is a good example of your essay's theme, then include it. If you are just including it because you think that you will impress the reader with everything you have ever done, think again.

Remember that scholarship committees want to know how resilient you are. While it is certainly okay to write about obstacles you have faced, what is important to your reader is how you overcame the obstacle, not what a terrible obstacle it was.

Do Not Make These Mistakes

Just as you should know what to do, you should also know what NOT to do! Here are some of the biggest blunders students make in their personal statement.

Mistake 1: Repeating information contained elsewhere in the application.

Here is an example of this type of mistake:
"In my junior year I was a cheerleader for my school. I worked hard at it, and found it to be fun and challenging. I was also part of my school's Kids in the Kitchen program, which helped to make food available to poor people in my community. Cheerleading and volunteer work kept me very busy. I spent approximately twenty hours each week cheering and another five hours volunteering. I learned a lot from this experience and can manage my time effectively and maintain a positive attitude in the face of adversity."

Mistake 2: Complaining about your circumstances rather than explaining them.

Here is an example of this type of mistake:
"Because my mother is a single parent, she has had to make a lot of sacrifices to keep me and my brother in a private school. It means that we have to go without many things, which is sometimes embarrassing. However, even though everyone in my school knows that we are poor, no one is willing to give me a break. This is especially true of my English teacher, Sister Magdalena. Because she didn't like me, and she is not comfortable with poor people, she gave me a C in English when I really should have gotten a B."

 **Mistake 3:** Discussing money or as a motivating factor for applying to a particular scholarship.

Yes, we all apply to scholarships to win money. In addition, we all want to win the most prestigious scholarships around. However, scholarship committees who read your personal statement want to know that you are motivated by a love of learning and contributing to the community. So, even though money or a scholarships' ranking may be important to you, keep this information out of your essay.

A "gimmicky" essay is one in which the writer tries to get the reader's attention through unconventional means. This does not mean that your essay has to follow one set format; what it means is that gimmicks cannot replace substance.

Locate Scholarships

The truth is that it is easy to find scholarships. When you decide to begin applying for scholarships, you will start to see scholarship opportunities all around. The best places to look for scholarships are

- ❏ The library
- ❏ Community colleges
- ❏ Magazines
- ❏ Newspapers
- ❏ The counselor's office
- ❏ Books
- ❏ The internet

Scholarships are listed in many names: academic awards, essay contests, promotions, even drawings. I have included a snapshot of my Fastweb account that shows many different types of scholarships. Remember - you can apply to all types of scholarships, but be sure to set goals.

Set Scholarship Goals

It is important that you set time aside - every week - to apply for scholarships. It is also important to identify the types of scholarships you will apply for. Do you have a lot of time to apply for scholarships? Consider entering a competition. Do you have a lot of homework in your English or History class? Consider entering an essay contest.

As you locate scholarships, it is most important that you set goals for applying to them. Having a goal sheet will help you to select scholarships to apply for and contests to enter. I have included the Scholarship Club monthly goal sheet for you. Use this goal sheet every month to identify the scholarships, contests, and promotions you will enter.

Scholarship Application Goal Sheet

Name: Date:

I will enter these Essay Contests

I will apply for these Scholarships

I will enter this science/math contest

My Notes

Evaluating Scholarship Opportunities

The next step in your scholarship PLAN is to make sure that the scholarships you apply for are worth it. You will spend a lot of time and energy finding scholarships, writing and re-writing essays, and submitting applications. Make sure that the scholarship you apply for is the best one for you.

As a Scholarship Coach, I work with dozens of students applying for local and national scholarships. Before I began Coaching, I witnessed students put a lot of effort into a national contest that only awards one scholarship. I also witnessed students apply for and win a scholarship only to have to return it because they did not read all of the details. The student did not realize that the scholarship was awarded for attending a specific university.

Over the years, I have developed a system for evaluating scholarship opportunities. We use this system at The Scholarship Club, and I always use it when I provide Scholarship Coaching. The system is based on the 10 most crucial attributes of any scholarship. In the next section you will learn to rank scholarships as "A", "B", or "C". Evaluating and ranking a scholarship will allow you to invest your time and effort where you will get the largest payoff. You will find that it is wise to spend your time working on "A" and "B" scholarships first and work on "C" scholarships only if you have extra time.

The 10 most crucial attributes of any scholarship opportunity are:

- Fit
- Competition
- Deadline
- Preparation
- Number of awards
- Amount of Award
- Renewability
- Auto-Renewability
- Portability
- Type of ongoing eligibility

Let us explore each of these attributes more closely.

Scholarship Fit

Fit refers to your eligibility for the scholarship. Ask yourself if you are a good candidate for this particular scholarship. If the scholarship is awarded to students interested in a certain profession or field of study, and you are interested in that field too, then the scholarship is a good fit for you. How can you tell if the scholarship is not a good fit for you? If the award is based on something, you are not interested in or based on a hobby that you have not started – do not apply. It is probably not a good fit for you.

Level of Competition

You will need to examine the type of competition for the scholarship. Is the scholarship a national competition? Is it local? Is the scholarship only for students who attend your high school or live in your city? In general, a scholarship with less competition is a better fit for you.

Scholarship Deadline

The deadline of the scholarship, when it's **Due,** will determine if you have a lot of time to prepare the application, or if you will have to rush. Depending on where you are in your high school career, and what your other activities are, a scholarship due in 2 weeks can be very good for you or very bad for you. Suppose you are a High School Senior studying for SAT's, preparing for Prom, and playing on the Volleyball team. The time you have available to prepare 3 to 4 drafts of an essay will be very limited. A 2-week deadline for a scholarship would be bad for you. On the other hand, suppose you are a High School Freshman with an essay due in 1 week. A 2-week deadline for a scholarship essay on the same topic as your school essay is very good for you. You will have your paper completed and submitted to your teacher *before* the scholarship deadline. This gives you plenty of time to submit the essay to the scholarship organization.

Preparation Required

The amount of preparation you will need to apply to a scholarship is important. If you already have your personal statement and letters of recommendation assembled, you will not need a lot of preparation time. Writing a report or performing an experiment for a scholarship will require a lot of preparation.

Number of awards

The number of scholarships awarded by an organization tells you a lot. The number of awards gives you an idea about your chances for winning. Some organizations, like Wal-Mart, give hundreds of scholarships to students. Other scholarships award to only 1 or 2 students. As a scholarship seeker, searching for opportunites from an organization that gives many awards is good.

Award Amount

The award amount refers to the dollar amount of the scholarship. The dollar amount is a good piece of information, but you must consider it like any of the other attributes. Sure, a $5000 award seems better than a $500 award. Nevertheless, if the organization is awarding three $5000 scholarships and another is awarding thirty $500 awards, the $500 scholarship may be better for you.

Renewability

Is this scholarship renewable; can you apply for or win the scholarship again next year? Scholarships that allow you to win more than once are good.

Auto- Renewability

Auto-Renewable scholarships are those that you can receive more than once; you will get the scholarship again next year. A good example is the Gates Millennium scholarship; it automatically renews every year for 4 years.

Portability

Is the scholarship portable? Portable means that you can use the scholarship at any school, or for any major you choose.

Type of ongoing eligibility

Ongoing eligibility describes what you have to do to keep the scholarship for more than 1 year. Do you have to play a certain sport? Do you have to maintain a certain GPA? Do you have to declare a certain major? In general, scholarships with ongoing eligibility are good.

Ranking Scholarship Opportunities

Scholarship opportunities are all around you. It is important to know which scholarship opportunity is best *for you.* At The Scholarship Club, we use a system for ranking every scholarship opportunity before we apply. We suggest that you rank each scholarship attribute on a scale from "1" to "3." "1" is the lowest score possible and "3" is the highest score possible. There are two exceptions; renewable or auto-renew. These two can get a rank of "0". The maximum points that any scholarship opportunity can score is "30" because there are 10 attributes with a maximum of 3 points each. Here is guidance on how to rank each item.

Eligibility or "Fit"

Are you a good candidate for this award? If the scholarship is a national award where anyone who breathes and goes to high school is a candidate, you should give it a **3** for fit. If it's an award with specific criteria and you don't exactly fit but you really want to "go for it," rank it **2 or 1.** If the scholarship is a highly specific award and you do not fit the eligibility criteria at all, rank it a **1.**

Competition

Who else can compete for this scholarship? National awards are open to everyone and should be ranked **1**. Regional or local awards will be less competitive based on the number of applicants, so it gets a rank of 2. If the award is specific to your city or your high school, rank it **3** because there won't be a lot of competition. For city and school-based scholarships there will be a small pool of students who can apply.

Deadline

We discussed earlier that the deadline, when it is **Due,** has to fit into the rest of your life. Rank the scholarship **3** if the deadline is months away. Rank it **2** if you have several weeks to submit your application. If the application deadline is this week, it gets a rank of **1**.

Preparation

Some scholarships require the standard items you will have in your Scholarship Application Kit; transcripts, essay, letters of recommendation. Rank the opportunity **1** if the scholarship requires a project or research report. Rank it **2** if it requires the standard Scholarship Application items. If you are working with a Scholarship Coach rank the scholarship **3**. The Scholarship Coach will make sure that you have enough time to prepare the application.

Number of Awards

The more awards given, the better your chance of to winning one of those awards. Use the following system as a way to rank this criterion.

- **1** for 1-4 awards
- **2** for 5-20 awards
- **3** for more than 20 awards

Amount of Award

Although every bit of money helps, it makes sense to focus more attention on a $5,000 award than on a $500 award. Use the following ranking system.

- **1** for awards up to $300
- **2** for awards between $300 - $3,000
- **3** for awards over $3,000

Pay close attention to awards that have "variable" amounts. Many times these scholarships can be "full tuition" awards.

Renewability

Renewable scholarships are those that you can win or receive again, you just have to re-apply. Use the following ranking system.

0 If the award is not renewable

3 if the award is renewable

Auto-Renewability

Auto-Renewable scholarships are those that you will automatically receive again next year. Use the following ranking system.

0 If the scholarship is not auto-renewable

3 if the scholarship is auto - renewable

Portability

Portable refers to where you can use the scholarship award. Use the following ranking system.

1 if you can use the scholarship at only one school

2 if you can use the award at a group of schools (HBCU's, etc)

3 if you can use the award at any school you choose

Ongoing Eligibility

Are there conditions for receiving this award year after year? Give the scholarship a rank of **1** if you must play a sport or have a certain major to keep it. Give it a rank of **2** if the scholarship eligibility is based on keeping a specific GPA. Rank the scholarship a **3** if it is awarded with no criteria (you just have to be in school and doing well).

Prioritize

Assign a point to each criterion, and then total the points for the scholarship. The Scholarship Club Ranking System will help you identify the best scholarships for you by showing you scholarship points.

A scholarship that has between **22 and 30 points is an "A"** Priority for you. You must apply for this scholarship!

A scholarship that scores between **15 and 21 points is a "B"** Priority for you. You should make time to apply for this scholarship.

A scholarship that scores between **7 and 14 points is a "C"** Priority for you. Apply for this scholarship if you have time *after* you have applied for the A and B scholarships. A scholarship that scores below 7 points is probably not worth your time.

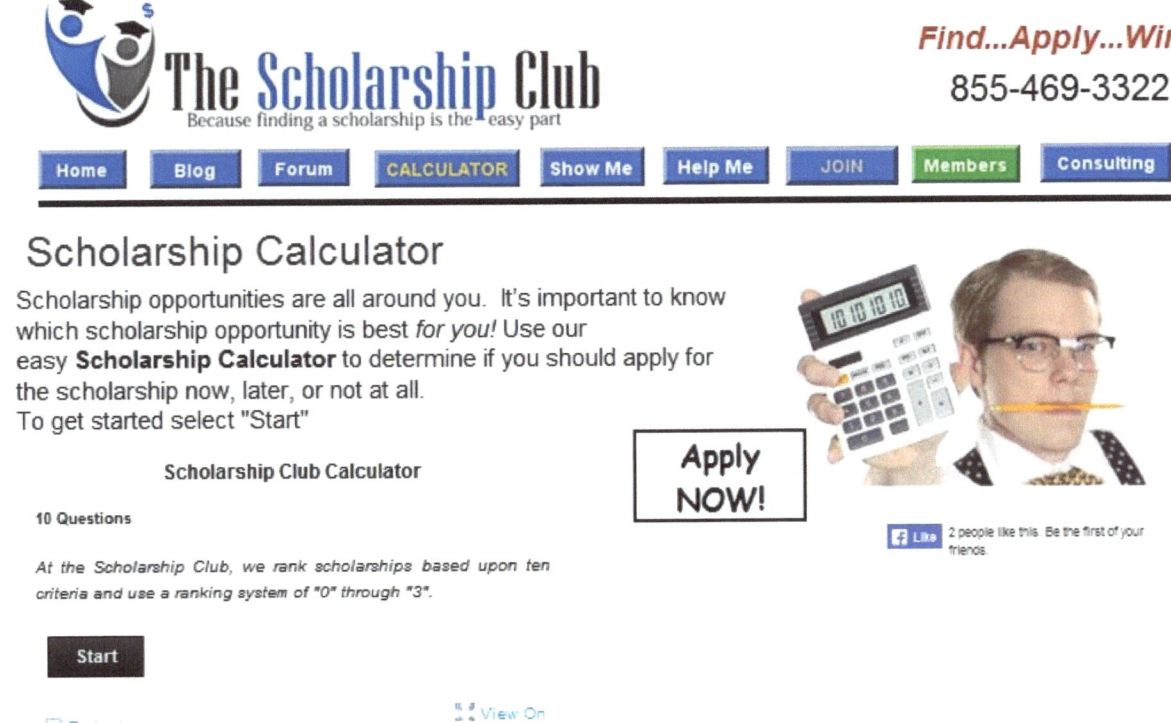

The Scholarship Club Ranking Tool

On the next page you will see a form that we have created to help you rank your scholarships. The form is quite handy, but it also takes a lot of time. After you have a clear understanding of how to rank a scholarship, I suggest you use our handy Scholarship Calculator located here:

http://scholarshipclub.homestead.com/Calculator.html

We created the Scholarship Calculator for our Scholarship Club members. You will notice that it can save you a lot of time while helping you decide on which scholarships to apply.

Use the **Scholarship Application Tracking Tool** that we have included on the following page. This tools will help you manage your scholarship applications.

The Scholarship Club
Scholarship Application Priority Tool

Scholarship	Fit	Competition	Deadline	Preparation	# of Awards	$$$	Renewable	Auto Renew	Portable	Ongoing eligibility	Total	Priority

Scholarship Application Tracking Tool
Use this tool to keep track of you scholarship applications

Scholarship Name	What did you turn in?	Due Date	Date you sent it in	Award Amount	Amount you won
Example: Discover Scholarship	Essay	October 1	September 15	$3000	$3000
			Totals		

Finding Scholarships

There are many places to find scholarship opportunities.

- ☐ Websites
- ☐ Internet Searches
- ☐ Local Colleges
- ☐ Career/Professional sites
- ☐ Local Businesses
- ☐ Magazines
- ☐ Newspapers

High schools and community colleges are often over looked sources for scholarship opportunities. In fact, your local community college will often have the widest variety of scholarships because community colleges support all levels of students; therefore, they provide information for each category of student. Magazines and newspapers will give you a lot of valuable information too, and it does not matter if they are print magazines or online newspapers.

Do not neglect to review Blogs and e-zines for scholarship information. These are great sources of information, usually written by people who have actually won scholarships. Blogs will often have "inside information" about the application process that you wouldn't ordinarily find on the "official" scholarship website. Once you have identified a scholarship opportunity, you must evaluate it to make sure that it is the right scholarship opportunity *for you*.

Applying for scholarships makes good economic sense. Suppose you enter a scholarship contest that awards $200 for writing an essay. Let's assume it takes you 8-hours to write 2 drafts and a final version. By winning that $200 scholarship, you have just earned $25 per hour. Do you know any job that pays a high school student $25 per hour? Do not forget that you have also received credit for your class assignment!

The following pages introduce **The Scholarship Club Class Leverage Sheet**. Use this sheet as a guide to ideas about how to leverage your homework for scholarships.

The Scholarship Club™
Class Leverage Sheet

Class Topic: US Economy

Class Themes: Borrowed from the website of George Thompson Nogales High School
http://www.nusd.k12.az.us/Schools/nhs/gthomson.class/

Record the major themes covered or discussed in your class on these lines

- **President Obama**
- **Bill of Rights**
- **Homework Assignment: Minimum Wage Position Paper**

Related Essay Contests:

Governor Charlie Crist's Black History Month Essay Contest
http://www.floridablackhistory.com/essay.cfm

"Barack Obama and Abraham Lincoln: Getting Right with Lincoln"
http://www.thelincolnforum.org/essayContest.html

The Progressive Economics Forum Student Essay Contest
http://www.progressive-economics.ca/student-essay-contest/

Scholarships:

Your Class Leverage Sheet

The Scholarship Club™

Class Leverage Sheet

Class Topic:

Class Themes:

Record the major themes covered or discussed in your class on these lines

Related Essay Contests:

Related Scholarships:

Build Your Scholarship Team

Applying for scholarships is a "Team Event." Sometimes your team members are other students applying for a scholarship with you. Many times the team is your system, people you will depend on as you go through this process.

Your "**First Team**" is made up of the people who can help you as you apply for scholarships. Your First Team members are:
- Parents
- Teachers
- Counselors
- Scholarship Coach
- Friends

Here is a description of what the members of your First Team will do.

Parents – help with researching scholarships, mail applications, drive you around to scholarship interviews, make phone calls while you are in school, proofread your essay/application, and provide overall encouragement.

Teachers – proofread your essays, make suggestions about what to write, give you information about local scholarships, listen to your concerns, and write letters of recommendation.

Counselors – forward scholarship information to you, help you get your transcript, talk with you about your academic goals, complete administrative reports, proofread your applications, and write letters of recommendation.

Scholarship Coach – help you determine which scholarships to apply for, maintain your scholarship application calendar, help you assemble your "tool kit", prepare you for scholarship interviews, proofread your applications, and provide encouragement.

Friends – help you remember what is important, listen to your concerns, provide a safe place to talk about your fears, and provide lots of encouragement.

Keep Track of Your Accomplishments

Recording your leadership activity and community service can be as easy as keeping a diary of the things you do in-and-outside of school. If you are not the "diary type," you can keep track of your leadership experience and community service activity on the logs we provided. Make sure that you remember where you file the log.

The Scholarship Club
Community Service Log

List the duties you performed

Date	Community Service Activity	Supervisor's Name (print)	Supervisor's Phone Number	Hours Worked

The Scholarship Club
Leadership Activity Log

List the duties you performed

Date	Project and Leadership Activity	Director's Name (print)	Director's Phone Number	Hours Worked

Locate Scholarships Online

Using the Internet to find scholarships is more than registering with free online scholarship databases; that is just the beginning. At The Scholarship Club, we teach a class called "Researching Scholarships Using the Internet." We usually start the class by talking about the myths regarding searching for scholarships. Myths like

- Everything you need to find scholarships is online
- Everything online is free
- It's easy to find exactly what you're looking for on the Internet

Finding the information you want on the Internet is like scuba diving, not like surfing. You have to be prepared to "go deep," stay focused on your task, and observe some safety rules.

When searching for scholarships on the Internet there are some things you should do, and some things you should not do.

You Should:
- Create a separate (free) email address just for your scholarship and college applications
- Include the correct zip code of your home/school when asked
- Fill out the interest survey completely

You <u>Should Not</u>:
- Provide your social security number or driver's license when *requesting* scholarship information
- Pay a fee to receive scholarship information or applications
- Include your phone number when *requesting* scholarship information

Internet Jargon

By now, you should know what a **search engine** is and what it does. A search engine is an information retrieval system that allows you to get specific information from the World Wide Web. The search engine allows you to ask for information that meets specific criteria and delivers a list of items that match your criteria. Popular search engines are
- Yahoo.com
- Google.com
- Ask.com
- Altavista.com

For a detailed list of search engines visit:

http://www.searchengineguide.com/searchengines.html

Some search engines are better for researching scholarships. You will find that there are search engines which are better for finding audio or music, search engines, which are better for finding images, even search engines that specialize in multimedia and video. When you are searching for scholarships using plain English, we recommend the following search engines:

>Google.com – www.google.com
>Ask.com – www.ask.com
>Hakia – www.hakia.com
>Live Search – www.live.com
>iSEEK Education - http://education.iseek.com

A **metasearch engine** reviews many search engines at the same time. Metasearch engines are very efficient when you are beginning your search. Many metasearch engines are **Second Generation** Internet search services. This means that these engines use a technology that organizes search results by peer ranking, clustering results by concept or group results by user behavior. Using this technology means that you will get more meaningful results.

The Metasearch engines we like are:

>www.ChunkIt.com   www.Mamma.com
>www.Dogpile.com   www.Ixquick.com
>www.BrainBoost.com   www.WebCrawler.com

We like these engines for a variety of reasons. The number 1 reason is that we can find scholarships by using them. In addition, the information is in a form you can use, not simply a long list of items. You will read a pre-view of the article or Blog before moving forward with the search. Many of these engines return documents that appear in the top 10 of any search result.

Discussion Questions:

Which search engines do you use most?
What metasearch engine will you try?

Scholarship Opportunities

Below you will find excellent free Internet resources for finding scholarships.

Fastweb – www.fastweb.com – A free membership-based scholarship database

Scholarship Experts – www.scholarshipexperts.com – A free membership-based scholarship database

FAFSA – www.fafsa.ed.gov – free Federal Application for Student Aid

Fed Money – www.fedmoney.org – A guide to government aid

Student Aid – http://studentaid.ed.gov – A government student aid on the web

GI Bill – www.gibill.va.gov – information about the GI Bill

Hispanic Scholarship Fund – www.hsf.net – scholarship opportunities and resources for Hispanic students

American Indian College Fund – www.collegefund.org – scholarships & resources for American Indians

Asian Pacific Fund – www.asiapacificfund.org/awards - scholarships for Asian students

United Negro College Fund – www.uncf.org – scholarships and resources for black students

Campus Pride – www.campuspride.org – resources for GLBT in college

Working With A Scholarship Coach

After working with students and parents for a few years, we noticed something. It seems that even though club members know what to do to win scholarships, many were not making time to apply! After our initial shock and amazement, we decided to offer scholarship coaching to help our busy students and parents.

A Scholarship Coach will help you organize your materials and get your scholarships completed and submitted on time. A Scholarship Coach **will not** apply for scholarships for you, write your essays, or guarantee that you will win any specific scholarship. Working with a Scholarship Coach will take much of the anxiety out of applying for scholarships by helping you focused and stay on track. The Coach will make sure that you are applying to scholarships that you qualify for (we have seen too many students apply for scholarships that do not work for them.) Here is a list of the ways in which a Scholarship Coach can help:

- Assist with researching scholarships early
- Evaluate Scholarship Opportunities
- Carefully review eligibility requirements
- Help organize all scholarship materials
- Help prepare for scholarship interviews
- Proofread applications carefully
- Ensure that no items are blank
- Ensure instructions are followed "to-the-letter"
- Make and maintain copies of everything
- Double-check the application

Your Scholarship Coach will help you develop a time-line for applying to scholarships, and will help you stick to the schedule. If you would like more information about getting a Scholarship coach, contact us at 855-469-3322.

Networking for Success

Getting "network smart" does not mean learning how to connect your computer to the Internet. You will want to develop skills in networking with people who share your interests and passions. **Networking** with others will allow you to share what you know, as well as get information that you may not otherwise have access to.

You can network online as well as in-person, and I recommend doing both. Networking online involves using many of the social-networking sites you probably already use. The difference is that you will use them to find scholarships as well as keep up with your friends. Using the Internet to network, this way is referred to as the **Social Web** that uses an Open Social platform. If you would like to know more about the technical side of Open Social applications you can check it out on Wikipedia at http://en.wikipedia.org/wiki/OpenSocial. I encourage you to join scholarship and study groups on your social networking sites. The next chapter gives a list of sites that use the Open Social platform and groups that can help you find scholarships.

In-person networking sites are great ways to find out about events that you are interested in. The site I have found to be most useful for this type of networking is meetup.com at http://www.meetup.com/. This networking site will allow you to find just about any type of group meeting for just about any type of purpose. It is free to register with meetup.com and you can join groups that meet in your neighborhood. If you live in southern California, you might want to check out these groups:

http://financialaid.meetup.com/15/
http://gradschool.meetup.com/46/
http://www.meetup.com/LA-Young-Pros/
http://www.meetup.com/10-Secrets-to-Creating-Exceptional-Students-Seminar/

Team Scholarships

Stuck at the Prom Scholarship – a couple can win up to $3000 for making their prom outfits out of duct tape and sending the photo to Duck Brand Duct Tape.
http://www.ducktapeclub.com/contests/prom/

Exploravision Science Competition – Groups of two, three or four K-12 students may enter the Exploravision Science Competition to explore technologies of the future. http://www.exploravision.org/

Team Scholarships for Law Enforcement - Team scholarships will provide interdisciplinary teams of four members the opportunity to train together at the conference. The SART team scholarship program is administered by the Sexual Assault Resource Service.
http://www.sartconference.com/Articles/Scholarships_files/Scholarships.pdf

Discovery Education 3M Young Scientist Challenge - In 2008 3M joined forces with Discovery Education in a quest to nurture the next generation of American scientists with an innovative and interactive science program open to every middle school student in America.
http://youngscientist.discoveryeducation.com/getstarted.html

One key to winning is to select a winning team and to continue entering contests with that team.

Contests and Competitions

http://youngscientist.discoveryeducation.com/
Mentioned in Chapter 5

http://www.heyugly.org/contests.php
Ages 10 – 19

http://homeschooling.gomilpitas.com/explore/contests.htm
Contests for home-schooled children

http://www.randomhouse.com/kids/writingcontests/#youngadult
Writing Contests for students aged 9 -12 and 12 -18

http://www.actionfornature.org/eco-hero/index.html
Ages 8 – 16

http://www.davidsongifted.org/fellows/
Students under age 18 interested in the Technology, Arts and Music

http://www.guardianlife.com/womens_channel/girls_going_places/girls_going_places.html
Girls ages 12 to 19

http://www.barronprize.org/nominate/index.html
Community service focused students aged 8 – 18

http://www.kohlscorporation.com/CommunityRelations/scholarship/index.asp
Community service focused students under age 21

http://mathcounts.org/Page.aspx?pid=195
Math competition for students

http://www.newscurrents.com/intro/edcartoons/carcon2.html
Art contests for students in K-6, 7-9, and 10 – 12

http://www.vfw.org/index.cfm?fa=cmty.leveld&did=151
VFW Patriots Pen contest

http://www.dosomething.org/awards
Awards for students under age 25

http://www.thinkquest.org/en/
Groups aged 19 and under, 15 & under, and 12 and under users conducting similar searches.

The College Application Process

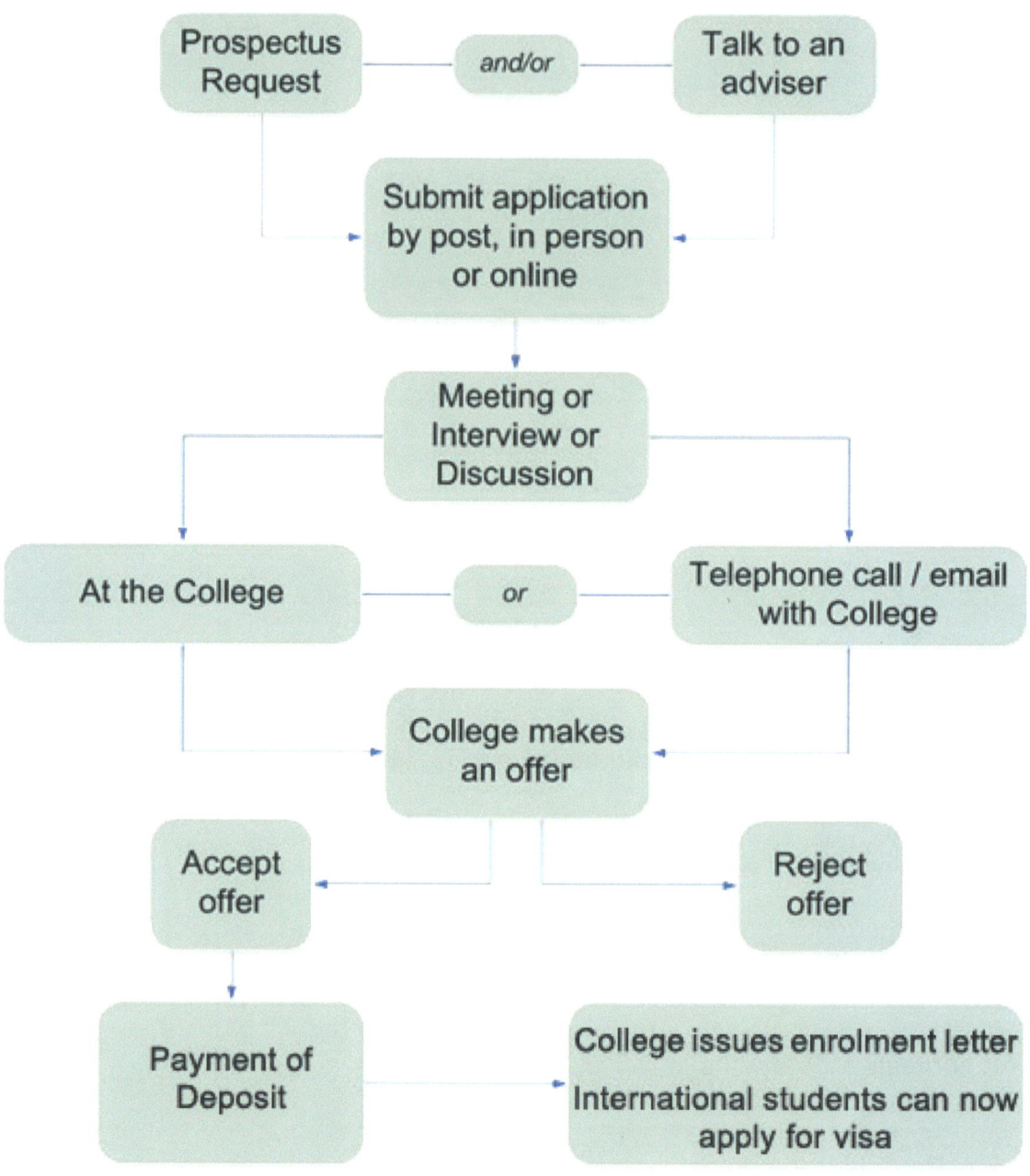

Developing a good understanding of the college application process will give you a "leg-up" in your scholarship search. You will understand that the college planning process, like winning scholarships, is something that you should start early in your high school career. Starting early means that you plan your extra-curricular activities and your summer events with college in mind. You want to select school clubs that interest you and join them. If the club is a good fit, plan to hold an office in it. Holding an office in a school club is one way to build your academic resume, and a way to get experience working with other students. **Club Officer** experience will serve you well on the college campus because you will be more comfortable about assuming a leadership position when you get to college.

Understanding the college application process will allow you to be aware of opportunities when they are presented to you. You will understand that attending a summer program in math or drama (if those are your areas of interest) will
1. Build your academic resume
2. Give you experiences that you can write about in scholarship essays
3. Show judges that you have interests outside of the classroom

If the idea of spending your summer in a "classroom" does not appeal to you, consider working during the summer. The work can be paid or volunteer, but it will give you experiences that you can talk about in your essays. Summer work can be related to your interests. Perhaps you like animals – you can work in a veterinarian's office for experience. If you live in an area with few jobs, consider volunteering. Volunteering is a wonderful way to get experience as you demonstrate your commitment to your community. In fact, I am a big fan of students working **and** volunteering during the summer.

Getting "College Smart" involves understanding as much about the college experience as you can. "College Smart" means thinking about all of the colleges you want to attend; think about attending graduate school now, before you begin your initial college career. Thinking about where you want to **end your college** career (with a Master's degree? With a PhD?) will help you decide where to begin your college career. You may decide to attend a college because it has the Graduate program you are interested in. You may decide that you do not want to have any college debt; in that case, you can choose one of the **15 colleges in the U.S. that offer free tuition.**

Getting smart about college involves finding out as much as you can about the colleges you are interested in. You will want to read articles about the college, visit the website of the college, take a virtual tour of the campus, and make an actual visit to the campus as well. Finding out about the college also means that you find out what the students on that campus think about the school. You can get student information from sites like Unigo or StudentsReview. You will read information written by students about topics like campus life, professors, dorm living, even the cafeteria food!

I suggest that you take the time to read student reviews. Be pro-active by calling the campus Career Center to ask for the contact information of **alumni**, and then call a few alum. When you visit the campus, be sure to tour to dormitories, the dining halls, the library, and the building of your major. Make time to speak with a department chairperson or the dean of the department.

Try to become an "expert" on the colleges you would like to attend. I have included a checklist of items to see during a campus visit; use the checklist when you take campus tours.

Discussion Questions:

Name three colleges/universities that you have an interest in.

Name three colleges/universities that you do not know now, but will research.

The Scholarship Club
College Visit Form

Name of College/University_____

Date of Visit:_____

Type of Institution_____   Tuition $_____

Visit Checklist

☐ Took a virtual tour   ☐ Toured the Dorms   ☐ Toured a classroom

☐ Took a physical tour   ☐ Toured a Dining Hall   ☐ Toured the Library

☐ Spoke to actual students   ☐ Spoke with Professor   ☐ Spoke w/Administrator

☐ Interviewed on campus   ☐ Talked with Admissions   ☐ Talked with Financial Aid

Talked with
  ○ Athletic Coach   ○ Band Director   ○ College Dean /Department Chair

Key Questions

What are the Strong Majors?_____

What are the Unique Programs? _____

What is this campus most known for? _____

What is the nearest City/Town?_____

How would you describe the students? _____

Are there any special academic requirements? _____

Does this campus "feel" comfortable to you? _____

What I like most about this campus:

What I like least about this campus:

College Planning Sites

College Surfing – www.collegesurfing.com – search for non-traditional colleges; career training, vocational, specialized.

College Mapper - https://www.collegemapper.com/ - guided tasks throughout the college planning process

Zinch – www.zinch.com – Facebook-like member site. Connects students and college administrators.

Government Education Info – www.students.gov/STUGOVWebApp/Public - government education info.

Embark – www.embark.com – create your own college plan.

Collegeboard – www.collegeboard.com – SAT registration and college information.

ACTstudent – www.ACTstudent.org – ACT registration and college information.

Xap – www.xap.com – free membership-based college planning site. Create your own college plan.

College Prowler - http://collegeprowler.com/ - college reviews written by students

GradSchool.com - http://www.gradschools.com/Subject/Urban-and-Regional-Planning/381.html - Free site with help in planning for Graduate School.

Number2.com - http://www.number2.com/ - Free test preparation for ACT, SAT and
GRE

National Center for Educational Statistics - http://nces.ed.gov/ - very official site.

TestPrepReview.com - http://www.testprepreview.com/ - Free test preparation for more than 50 college and vocational exams

Discussion Question:

Which College Planning site will you access?

"Free Tuition" Colleges

Alice Lloyd College - http://www.alc.edu/

Berea College - http://www.berea.edu/

Barclay College - www.barclaycollege.edu/

College of the Ozarks - http://www.cofo.edu/

Cooper Union - http://www.cooper.edu/index2.html

Curtis Institute of Music - http://www.curtis.edu/html/10000.shtml

Deep Springs College - http://www.deepsprings.edu/home

Franklin W. Olin College of Engineering - http://www.olin.edu/

St. Louis Christian College - https://www.slcconline.edu

US Air Force Academy - http://www.usafa.af.mil/index.cfm?catname=AFA%20Homepage

US Coast Guard Academy - http://www.cga.edu/display.aspx?id=329

US Merchant Marine Academy - http://www.usmma.edu/

US Military Academy (West Point) - http://www.usma.edu/about.asp

US Naval Academy - http://www.usna.edu/Admissions/aboutusna.htm

Webb Institute of Naval Architecture - http://www.webb-institute.edu/

William E Macauley Honors College at CUNY – www.macaulay.cuny.edu/

Williamson Free School of Mechanical Trades – www.williamson.edu/

Discussion Question:

Which tuition free colleges would you consider attending?

Colleges That Recognize Talented "B" Students

Tamara Orr is author of **America's Best Colleges for B Students: A College Guide for Students without Straight A's**, a book I recommend. I have listed a few colleges that you may want to research further.

Assumption College	Albertson College	Azusa Pacific
Albright College	Adelphi University	Bradley
Bowling Green	Bridgewater	Bryant University
Campbell	Carroll College, MT	Christopher-Newport
Chapman	Champlain College	Coastal Carolina
Coe College	Concordia University	College of Notre Dame
Coppin State U.	CU Boulder	CUNY Staten Island
Denver University	Elmira College	Endicott College
Earlham College	Florida State	Fort Lewis College
Gordon College	Gustavus Adolphus	Hartwick College
Hollins University	Lake Forest	Lebanon-Valley
Lenoir Rhyne College	Linfield College	Longwood
Long Island University	Loyola Marymount	Maine Maritime Academy
Marist College	Menlo College	Morgan State U.
Muskingham College	Norfolk State	Norwich University
Old Dominion	Ohio Northern	Pacific Lutheran
Pacific University	Quinnipiac University	Radford
Regis College	Roanoke College	Roger Williams U.
Springfield College	Shepard	Shenandoah
Southern Oregon U.	St. Joseph's	St. Lawrence
St. Mary's	Univ. of the Pacific	Univ. of Portland
U MD-Eastern Shore	Univ. of New England	Univ. of Redlands
Univ. Rhode Island	Univ. South Carolina	Univ. of San Diego
Univ. of San Francisco	Univ. of St. Thomas (MN)	Univ. of The Pacific
Univ. Vermont	Unity College	Utica College
Wagner College	Washington & Jefferson	Western New England
Whittier College	Xavier College (OH)	VCU

Extraordinary College Info Sites

This page offers information on exceptional colleges alongs with other great sites for researching colleges and scholarships that are right for you.

Colleges That Change Lives – www.ctcl.org. A site listing unique colleges.

Youniversity – www.youniversity.tv. This site features virtual campus tours.

Government College Search – http://nces.ed.gov/collegenavigator. College search site.

College View – www.collegeview.com. A College search site.

USnews – www.usnews.com. This site lists national college rankings.

Merit Aid – www.meritaid.com. This site features colleges with offer merit based aid.

Ucan – www.ucan-network.org. A directory of private schools.

A to Z colleges – www.a2zcolleges.com. School and degree information for students seeking advanced degrees.

Catholic Colleges – www.catholiccollegesonline.org. A site for searching for catholic colleges.

College Living Experience – www.cleinc.net. This site identifies college programs for students with disabilities.

Work College – www.workcolleges.org. Features information about the 6 work colleges that include work as part of the curriculum.

eLearners – www.ELearners.com. Assistance with finding online degrees

International Graduate Schools - http://www.careerowl.ca/ - lists international programs alphabetically by name

Get Career Smart

Get "Career Smart" by thinking about the type of job you would like to have. I encourage you to think beyond a job title; think about the type of life you would like to have.

Begin asking yourself questions such as "Do I want to work inside or out-doors?" "Do I want to work all year around?" "Do I want to have lots of vacation time in the summer?" "What's more important to me – the work I do or how many people I can help?"

You are going to have to know yourself well to be able to answer the questions above. Start getting to know yourself by taking time to think about the type of life you want. Take a personality test such as a Myers – Briggs style assessment. Begin to think about your personality style and the types of jobs that work well for your personality. The career search sites are free resource that can get you started with learning your personality style. I encourage you to take a learning style assessment too. It is important to know how you take-in information. This knowledge will help you choose a successful career path.

After you have spent some time learning your personality style and learning style, begin researching the types of careers that work well with your personality. Knowing the type of career that works well for you will help you choose a college major that you will enjoy, and will give you a head start on looking at scholarships for your major and your career.

Did you know that you could apply for a scholarship in a career that interests you now, before you even start college? There are scholarships for students interested in a career in science, engineering, law, journalism, accounting, teaching, research, medicine, allied health fields, management, marketing, childcare, veterinary medicine, social work, the military, social services, even Zoology.

Career Search Sites

Jung Typology Test – www.humanmetrics.com/#Jung%20Myers-Briggs. A free online Myers Briggs assessment.

www.personalitypage.com. Information about various personality types.

Occupational Outlook Handbook – www.bls.gov/oco/. Offers Information about job requirements, prospects, market conditions etc., for select jobs.

O*Net Resource Center – www.onetcenter.org/WIL.html. Offers printable assessments.

Quintessential Careers – www.quintcareers.com. Resources and tools for locating new jobs.

College Grad - www.collegegrad.com. Offers career assistance for recent college graduates.

The Career Project – http://www.thecareerproject.org Learn about thousands of jobs directly from the people who work them. Thousands of *career* profiles, free.

My Future – www.myfuture.com. A resource for finding careers right out of high school.

Myclubmylife – http://www.myclubmylife.com – Website content is always appropriate for teens, and is designed to help educate teens about career and education opportunities, healthy living, finances and much more in fun, interactive ways.

A Word About The Deep Web

You may have heard the term "deep web' used on the Internet or on TV. It's not some super-secret website reserved for finding questionable material, the term actually refers to how information is stored in this area of the World Wide Web. The deep web is sometimes called the "invisible web." The name comes from the idea that the information in this space is stored in databases, and you have to know how to ask the right question to get the information you want.

The information you will find stored in the deep web usually comes in list form, and is often **dynamic** or changing constantly. Here is list of the type of information you find in deep web databases:

- Phone books
- News
- Digital exhibits
- Job postings
- Airline flight information

You can use the deep web to search for scholarships, but you do not need to. There are many excellent search engines and metasearch engines that will provide the information you need.

Discussion Questions:

Have you heard about the deep web (before now)?

How is the deep web different from the Web?

Outstanding Searches

Below you will find some great search engines to use for finding scholarships. If you would like to learn more about detailed Internet search techniques and using Boolean logic, we offer a class called *Researching Scholarships Using the Internet*. For more information about this course just send us an email at schlolarlead@gmail.com.

AllTheWeb - returns results quickly from an extremely large database gathered by the Yahoo crawler; offers multimedia and news searches; has a good advanced search interface.

Ask.com - general search engine enhanced by a number of specialty searches including a dictionary, thesaurus, currency converter, encyclopedia, maps, news and more.

BananaSlug - uses the Google search mechanism and seeds your search with a random word from the category of your choice to return unusual results.

ChaCha - search engine that offers live human guides to help answer queries.

Dogpile - Dogpile is a search engine that fetches results from Google, Yahoo! and Yandex, and includes results from several other popular search engines

Duck Duck Go - offers disambiguation prompts (helps to clarify what question you are really asking)

Mahalo - A 'human-powered' search site in this list, employing a committee of editors to manually sift and vet thousands of pieces of content

Mamma - retrieves results from approximately a dozen major Internet search engines and directories

Ixquick – the worlds most private metasearch engine

Yippy - A Deep Web engine that searches other search engines for you

OpenSocial and Web 2.0

Ok, so I have to give you a little information about the differences between Web 2.0 and Open Social. I am a PhD student in Information Systems; the "teacher in me" will not let me skip this part (smile).

Web 2.0 begins with the idea of information being open – no one person "owns" the information. In the "old days" of Web 1.0, information was available at specific locations, many times for a fee. Think of the old "Britannica" encyclopedias. You could buy an encyclopedia, or you can subscribe to the Britannica site for a fee. In Web 2.0, no one "owns" the information; you can go to Wikipedia free and research just about any topic available today. Web 2.0 is characterized by two-way communication. Remember when personal websites were popular? Someone would purchase a site name and put content on it for anyone to read. That was web 1.0 – one-way communication. Today many people have Blogs; sites on which they put information, but allow them also you to ask questions or post responses to what you read. Blogs are Web 2.0

OpenSocial is a concept that involves software tools which allow you to socialize with people in different software applications. You use OpenSocial applications when you use the widgets and apps on Facebook. Most often, you will use OpenSocial on social networking sites that allow you to talk with other people, post to a forum, blog, etc. Social networking sites allow you to connect with other people to discuss many different topics, including how to find scholarships. We have listed some social networking sites that you can use to find scholarship information and discussions. Many times, you can just go to the site and type in "Scholarships" to find out who is talking about them.

- www.Ning.com
- www.equals6.com
- www.Facebook.com
- www.Blogger.com
- www.Youtube.com
- www.groups.yahoo.com
- www.google.com/edu/scholarships
- www.Linkedin.com

More Sites

Active Minds - http://www.activeminds.org/about A Leading nonprofit organization that empowers students to speak openly about mental health in order to educate others and encourage help-seeking.

Art Schools – www.artschools.com. A resource for students interested in studying any form of art or art history.

Bridge to Music – www.bridgetomusic.com. A music and music-career oriented website.

College Moms – http://www.collegeformoms.com/ A resource for mothers attending college.

Early Entrance Foundation – www.earlyentrancefoundation.org. An organization that helps gifted student's ages 11-15 enter college.

Education USA – http://educationusa.state.gov/. Information about student visas to study in the US.

EduPass – www.edupass.org. A resource for international students.

GI Bill – www.gibill.va.gov. Information about the GI Bill.

New Mobility – www.newmobility.com. Resources for wheel-chair-bound students.

GradView.com - http://www.gradview.com/index.jsp - Search for graduate schools by program, by city or by state.

ULifeline - http://www.ulifeline.org/ An anonymous, confidential, online resource center, where you can be comfortable searching for the information regarding emotional health.

Resources for Minority/Diverse Students

American Indian College Fund – www.collegefund.org. Scholarships & resources for American Indians.

Asian Nation – www.asian-nation.org. This site features discussions, articles, and blogs by, for, and about Asian students.

Asian Pacific Fund – www.asiapacificfund.org/awards - Scholarships for Asian students.

Black Excel – www.blackexcel.org. A college help network for black, minority students to gain admission and scholarships to college.

Black News – http://blackstudents.blacknews.com. Articles and scholarship & internship information for Black students.

Campus Pride – www.campuspride.org. Resources for GLBT in college.

College Horizons – www.collegehorizons.org. College preparation information for Native American students.

Congressional Hispanic Caucus Institute – www.chci.org/chciyouth-index. Site dedicated to developing the next generation of Latino leaders.

Gay Lesbian Straight Education Network – www.glsen.org. Resources for GLBT students at all schools (middle school, high school, and college).

Gay Straight Alliance – www.gsanetwork.org. This site connects campus organizations with resources.

Hillel – www.hillel.org. Resources for Jewish students regarding Jewish campus life.

Hispanic Fund – www.hispanicfund.org. Resources for Hispanic students.

Hispanic Scholarship Fund – www.hsf.net. Scholarship opportunities and resources for Hispanic students.

Korean American Scholarship Foundation - www.kasf.org – Resources for Korean American students

LBGT Campus – www.lgbtcampus.org. Resources for graduate students, faculty, and alumni regarding LBGT community.

MALDEF – www.maldef.org. Mexican American Legal Defense and Education Fund, scholarships and resources for Hispanic and students without legal status.

Posse – www.possefoundation.org. The Posse Foundation identifies, recruits, and trains incredible youth leaders from urban public high schools and sends these groups as "Posses" to top colleges and universities in this country.

Quest bridge – www.questbridge.org. A non-profit program that links bright, motivated low-income students with educational and scholarship opportunities at some of the nation's best colleges.

United Negro College Fund – www.uncf.org. Scholarships and resources for Black students.

Resources for Student Athletes and Parents

Be Recruited – http://colleges.berecruited.com/cgi-bin/schoolprofile.pl. This site connects athletes with college coaches.

College Student Athletes – www.collegestudentathletes.com. Allows a student to search NCAA III schools.

Joq Toq - www.joqtoq.com. A student athlete blog with resources.

Mom's Team – www.momsteam.com. Provides information and resources for the parents of athletes.

NAIA – http://naia.cstu.com. National Association of Intercollegiate Athletics, NAIA schools & resources.

NCAA Eligibility Center – http://web1.ncaa.org/eligibilitycenter/common. Lists eligibility requirements for NCAA division I or II students.

NCAA website – www.ncaastudent.org. Provides information about NCAA for transitioning students.

NJCAA – www.njcaa.org. National Junior College Athletic Association, resources for JC athletes.

Women's Sports Foundation – www.womenssportsfoundation.com. Provides resources for female athletes.

Resources for Students with Disabilities

Adaptive Environments – http://adaptiveenvironments.org/neada/site/education. This site lists information and resources for students including video of people with LD sharing their success stories.

Ahead – www.ahead.org. Association of Higher Education & Disabilities with resources and information for students.

Do It - http://www.washington.edu/doit/can-students-intellectual-disabilities-attend-college Students with intellectual disabilities attend college successfully.

Government Resources – www.disabilityinfo.gov. Information about rights and laws regarding people with disabilities.

NCLD – www.ncld.og. National Center for Learning Disabilities. Includes resources and information for students with learning disabilities.

Smart Kids – www.smartkidswithLD.org. This site offers help for parents to advocate for their children with Learning Disabilities.

Teacch – www.teacch.com/college.html. Resources for students who have autism or a communication disability.

Think College - http://www.thinkcollege.net/   College options for people with Intellectual Disabilities

College Diabetes Network - https://collegediabetesnetwork.org/ Resources for students juggling diabetes and college.

Lupus Inspiration Foundation for Excellence - http://www.lifescholarship.org/ This website provides resources for college students with lupus

Understood - https://www.understood.org/en/school-learning/choosing-changing-schools/leaving-high-school/9-steps-for-easing-the-transition-to-college Resources for students with learning and attention issues.

College Academic Support - http://collegeacademicsupport.com/ Website that provides resources to help students prepare for the transition from high school to college.

By now you've learned everything you need to know to begin applying for scholarships while you're still in High School. You'll need create your Scholarship Application Pack, get a calendar, start applying for scholarships, prepare for the interviews, and send a "Thank You" note after each interview. Here's a review of what you need in your **Scholarship Application Pack**:

1. **Scholarship Tool Kit** containing
    - A copy of your transcript
    - Academic Resume
    - Autobiographical essay
    - Letters of Recommendation
    - Log of leadership activities
    - Log of community service activities
    - Monthly goal sheets
    - Personal statement
    - Scholarship tacking tool
2. **A list of your First Team members**
3. **Class Leverage Sheets**
4. **Free Scholarship Profiles**
5. **College Visit Forms**
6. **Calendar** to keep track of:
    - Scholarship application deadlines
    - Recommendation due dates
    - Essay due dates
    - When items are mailed
    - Interview appointments
    - College visit dates

Now that you know what to do, you just need to do it! Here are some tips for making sure that you apply for scholarships:

1. Set aside time **every week** to review your scholarship accounts
2. Commit to a day and time **each month** to complete scholarship applications

3. Use the free resources listed in this e-book
4. Attend the free monthly Scholarship Club meetings
5. Watch the Scholarship Club videos on YouTube
6. Subscribe to our weekly newsletter by emailing us at Scholarlead@gmail.com
7. Identify who you want to be on your team
8. Share your scholarship search with your teachers and counselors
9. Don't wait to get help – start early looking for those who can help you find scholarships
10. Don't get discouraged if you don't win a scholarship the first time, take time to review your applications if you don't win.
11. Try to apply for 10 scholarships, essay contests, or academic competitions each month
12. Establish a savings account where you will keep your scholarship winnings

If you have any questions, feel free to contact us at The Scholarship Club at 855-469-3322 or on our website at www.TheScholarshipClub.com. You can always email me directly at ScholarLead@gmail.com.

Many other students have won scholarships while they are still in High School and you can too! The key is to get started and to stick with it. I wish you much success.

Great Success to You!

About The Scholarship Club FPC

Founded in 2008, The Scholarship Club is a scholarship coaching company that provides tools, resources and support to college bound students (and their parents or guardians) who are interested in obtaining scholarships to finance their college education. The Scholarship Club FPC offers one-on-one scholarship coaching to help students find the right scholarships, apply for and win money for college.

Rondalynne McClintock M.Ed, founder and CEO of The Scholarship Club FPC, knows firsthand what it's like to be a parent seeking information about scholarships. The idea of a scholarship club began when, hoping to alleviate the high cost of a college education for her daughter Talia, Rondalynne began a scholarship search. The Scholarship Club was created based on her personal journey.

When Talia was a high school junior, Rondalynne set out to find scholarships. She quickly realized there was a lot to know about the scholarship process. She scoured the Internet for hours on end. While there was a wealth of information, some of it was conflicting and ultimately confusing. Rondalynne organized key information, developed effective steps and strategies and helped Talia apply for eight scholarships. Talia won them all and the money was enough to cover most of the four-year tuition at Washington University, a private teaching and research university in St. Louis, MO. To help friends and church members who wanted to achieve the same success with scholarships, Rondalynne began a study group in her home. Word spread and the size of the group doubled, so meetings were moved to a church and later online. In 2008, the scholarship "study group" became The Scholarship Club.

Talia Dotson, now a college graduate and scholarship success story, is the Director of The Scholarship Club FPC. To date, members of The Scholarship Club have obtained college scholarships worth thousands of dollars. With scholarship coaching from The Scholarship Club, you too can win college scholarships. To find out more, call 855-469-3322.

www.ingramcontent.com/pod-product-compliance
Lightning Source LLC
Chambersburg PA
CBHW041519220426
43667CB00002B/37